Christmas

LABURNUM
PRESS

Katie Dicker

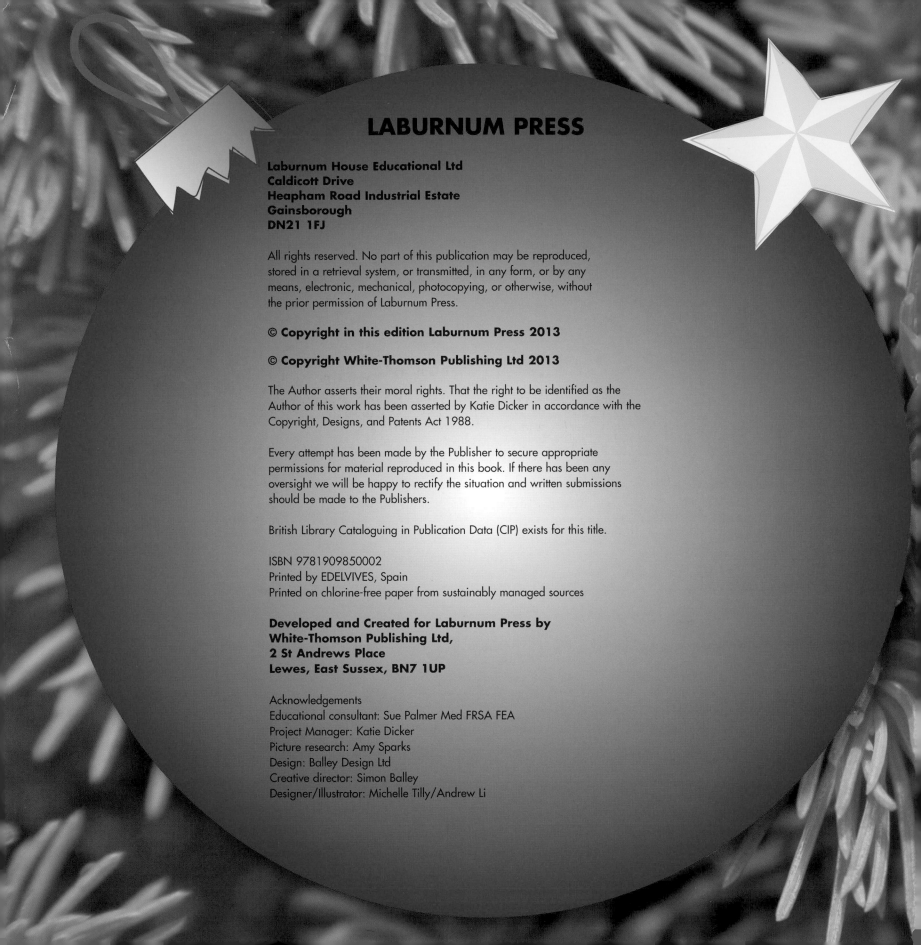

LABURNUM PRESS

Laburnum House Educational Ltd
Caldicott Drive
Heapham Road Industrial Estate
Gainsborough
DN21 1FJ

British Library Cataloguing in Publication Data (CIP) exists for this title.

ISBN 9781909850002
Printed by EDELVIVES, Spain
Printed on chlorine-free paper from sustainably managed sources

Developed and Created for Laburnum Press by
White-Thomson Publishing Ltd,
2 St Andrews Place
Lewes, East Sussex, BN7 1UP

Acknowledgements
Educational consultant: Sue Palmer Med FRSA FEA
Project Manager: Katie Dicker
Picture research: Amy Sparks
Design: Balley Design Ltd
Creative director: Simon Balley
Designer/Illustrator: Michelle Tilly/Andrew Li

Contents

A special birthday..............4

Church celebrations..........6

Christmas songs...............8

Countdown!...................10

Time to decorate.............12

Getting ready.................14

Surprise gifts..................16

Family feast...................18

Christmas worldwide.......20

Notes for adults..............22

Index 24

A Special birthday

twinkle!

Long ago, a bright star

led people to baby Jesus.

Today, we put on plays at Christmas to celebrate the birth of Jesus.

5

Church celebrations

star

This church is FULL

for a Christmas celebration.

6

OFFERT PAR LE 4ÈME PÈLERINAGE
DE PÉNITENCE . FRANCE . 1885

You can see the Christmas story in the stained glass windows.

Christmas songs

Noel, Noel!

These children are singing Christmas carols in the street.

8

What Christmas carols can YOU sing?

Away in a manger...

An advent calendar helps us to count the days until Christmas.

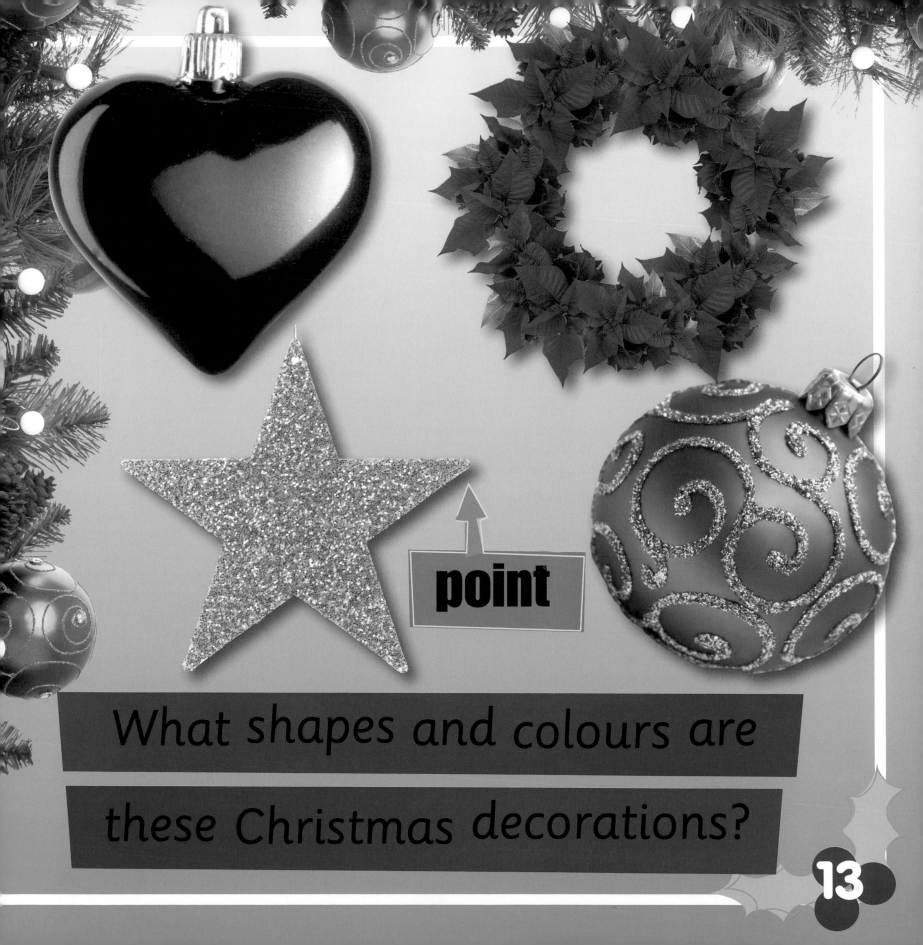

point

What shapes and colours are these Christmas decorations?

Getting ready

ribbon

What present shapes are easy to wrap?

14

Surprise gifts

squeeeze!

What presents fit

inside a stocking?

Pull!

At Christmas dinner, we share the crackers.

17

Family feast

sizzle!

How do YOUR family prepare the turkey?

prickle

Can you name some of these Christmas desserts?

19

In Germany, there are markets in the snowy streets at Christmas.

Welcome!

Sparklers books are designed to support and extend the learning of young children. The **Food We Eat** titles won a Practical Pre-School Silver Award, the **Body Moves** titles won a Practical Pre-School Gold Award and the **Out and About** titles won the 2009 Practical Pre-School Gold Overall Winner Award. The books' high-interest subjects link in to the Early Years curriculum and beyond. Find out more about Early Years and reading with children from the National Literacy Trust (www.literacytrust.org.uk).

Themed titles
Christmas is one of four **Celebrations** titles that encourage children to learn about annual festivals and different cultures around the world. The other titles are:
Easter   *Divali*   *Chinese New Year*

Areas of learning
Each **Celebrations** title helps to support the following Early Years Foundation Stage areas of learning:
Personal, Social and Emotional Development
Communication, Language and Literacy
Problem Solving, Reasoning and Numeracy
Knowledge and Understanding of the World
Physical Development
Creative Development

Making the most of reading time
When reading with younger children, take time to explore the pictures together. Ask children to find, identify, count or describe different objects. Point out colours and textures. Allow quiet spaces in your reading so that children can ask questions or repeat your words. Try pausing mid-sentence so that children can predict the next word. This sort of participation develops early reading skills.

Follow the words with your finger as you read. The main text is in Infant Sassoon, a clear, friendly font designed for children learning to read and write. The labels and sound effects add fun and give the opportunity to distinguish between levels of communication. Where appropriate, labels, sound effects or main text may be presented phonically. Encourage children to imitate the sounds.

As you read the book, you can also take the opportunity to talk about the book itself with appropriate vocabulary such as "page", "cover", "back", "front", "photograph", "label" and "page number".

You can also extend children's learning by using the books as a springboard for discussion and further activities. There are a few suggestions on the facing page. The Internet also has many teaching resources about annual festivals. For example, see www.365celebration.com and www.underfives.co.uk.

Pages 4–5: A special birthday

Talk to children about the Christmas story. You could put on a nativity play to hone their understanding or make a model nativity scene. Encourage children to remember and celebrate each other's birthdays. Display a list of the children's birthdays on the wall. Whose birthday is closest to 25 December?

Pages 6–7: Church celebrations

Explain to children that Christmas is a Christian celebration. Organise a visit to your local church. What does the inside of the church look and feel like? What sounds can the children hear? Children may also enjoy making their own stained glass windows from card and coloured film. What parts of the Christmas story can they illustrate?

Pages 8–9: Christmas songs

Help children to learn a Christmas carol. What part of the Christmas story are they singing about? Are there any actions the children can do while they sing? Children may also enjoy putting on a Christmas concert or carol singing to others.

Pages 10–11: Countdown!

Children may enjoy making a simple advent calendar, with opening windows or paper pockets. You could also make marks on a plain candle and safely burn it each day. Encourage children to count the days until Christmas. How many days are there in a week? How many weeks are there in a month?

Pages 12–13: Time to decorate

Help children to make their own Christmas decorations. You could make a star from lollipop sticks, for example, and sprinkle with glitter, or cut out paper hand shapes to make a circular wreath. Use the children's creations to decorate a Christmas tree or a branched twig. What shapes and colours are often used for Christmas decorations?

Pages 14–15: Getting ready

Explain to children that because Jesus was a gift to the world, we now give gifts to each other at Christmas. Help children to wrap different shapes and tie them with ribbons. Children may also enjoy making and writing their own Christmas cards. You could set up a model post office for children to act out a role play. Can the children measure and weigh the cards and parcels they are sending?

Pages 16–17: Surprise gifts

Children may enjoy playing the 'feely' game. Wrap some small items and put them in a stocking. Ask children to pick a present in turn and to describe what it feels like. When they unwrap the present, are their guesses correct? Encourage children to write a letter to Father Christmas. Children may also enjoy making a Christmas cracker or party hat.

Pages 18–19: Family feast

Help children to make their own mince pies using ready-made pastry and vegetarian mincemeat. What shapes can the children make for the pastry tops? Children may also enjoy making place mats and writing place names, for a tea party.

Pages 20–21: Christmas worldwide

Explain to children that Christmas is celebrated around the world, but not by everyone. Encourage children to talk about how their family celebrate Christmas (or another festival). Make a collage to illustrate different Christmas traditions around the world. Use the Internet to help you. Some examples include eating fish in Italy on Christmas Eve, kangaroos pulling Santa's sleigh in Australia and making an advent calendar with oranges and cloves in Norway.

Index

a

advent calendar **11**
advent candle **10**
Australia **21**

c

cards **15**
carols **8, 9**
celebration **5, 6, 7**
Christmas story **4, 5, 7**
Christmas tree **12, 21**
church **6, 7**
crackers **17**

d

decorations **12, 13, 21**

f

food **17, 18, 19**

g

Germany **20**

j

Jesus **4, 5**
Joseph **5**

m

markets **20**
Mary **5**

p

plays **5**
presents **14**

s

stained glass windows **7**
star **4, 6, 12, 13**
stocking **16**

Picture acknowledgements:
Alamy: 6 (Paul Rapson); **Corbis:** 5 (Image Source), 8 (Adam Woolfitt), 14 (JGI/Blend Images), 18 (Jose Luis Pelaez, Inc./Blend Images); **Dreamstime:** 2-3 pine needles (Spencer Berger), 11 teddy (Wan Rosli Wan Othman), 11 candy pole (Richard Cote), 11 toy soldier (Ron Chapple Studios), 22-23 pine needles (Spencer Berger), 24 pine needles (Spencer Berger); **Getty Images:** cover (Sean Justice), 9 (Frank Herholdt), 10 (Westend61), 12 (Andersen Ross), 15 (BLOOMimage), 16 (Sean Justice), 17 (Dylan Ellis), 21 (Bec Parsons); **IStockphoto:** 4 (Shane Illustration & Design), 13 tinsel (Barbara Helgason photography), 19 mince pie (Freelancebloke); **Photolibrary:** 11 (Image Source), 20 (Wolfgang Weinhäupl); **Shutterstock:** 7 (Zvonimir Atletic), 13 heart bauble (Vlad Ageshin), 13 wreath (Danylchenko Iaroslav), 13 star (Smileus), 13 green bauble (Planner), 19 yule log (Christopher Elwell), 19 panettone (Luiz Rocha), 19 christmas pudding (Christopher Elwell).